THIS

BOOK

BELONGS

to

__ __ __ __ __ __

because all names are six letters or less
unless you are called Johndrew.

STEVE BOBSON
EX LIBRIS MODERATOR

1

TO ALL STEVES,

We haven't met all of you yet.

'An absolute masterpiece, better than Macbeth'
- **Yelaf Spugdomery, Failed Poet**

'I read this twice without blinking to be quite frank, and it's not because it was short. It was quite frankly a blast'
- **Frank, Author of 'Frankly Frank'**

'I shlike this shbook, it's got a shboom to it that shno other shpoetry shbooks have. I love this shbook.'

-Shbing Shbang, 'Schtick Weekly'

'Haven't read it yet but since the authors are paying me to review it, I'll just say it's a good book.'
- **John, British Citizen**

'*Chiasmus* was a grate book, and here we are with the follow up. It has all the charm of the first book, but with an added layer of butter. With crisp new poems, I would chip in and grab it. It's very sweet, so if you're fishing for a new great book, take this one away!'
- **Mary Berry,** Winner of **Strictly Come Dining**

CON USION iS <u>an</u>
 F
        ART

CONTENTS

1. The Strange Events Collection

2. The Interpretation Collection

3. The Mundane Daily Experience Collection

CONTENTS

4. The Food Collection

5. The Brummie Collection

6. The Grand Collection

7. The Problems Collection

CONTENTS

8. The Illustrated Collection

9. The Animal Collection

10. The Sit Yourself Back And Relax Because There's A Lot To Read Collection

CONTENTS

11. Collection of some Importance

Page of Reflection

Use this page to reflect on life

Do you see yourself?

POEMS THAT PROBABLY SHOULDN'T EXIST

By Dhiran Sodha and Oliver Clarke

THE STRANGE EVENTS
COLLECTION

Prank

My friend said the toilet was to the left,
But it was to the right.
I learnt my lesson,
When I walked in;
And my gender was not apparent.

For in fact,
I could not find a place to go,
That was not seated,
And there were women
Within.

Did you hear?

Did you hear,
About Scotland?
They're selling all their mountains to England.

Did you hear about India?
They're changing their shape,
It's going to be less pointy.

Did you hear about France?
They're going to sell Paris to Argentina,
It's going to move next to Mendoza.

Did you hear about Japan?
They're selling all their earthquakes to Canada.

Did you hear about Jamaica?
They're selling their accent to Mexico,
And Poland are buying a new ocean.

The Sun

I stared at it,
It stared back at me,
I couldn't see,
The sand or the sea.

My eyesight fiee,
As Galileo Galilei,
Teach me that hath,
Not met me,
The sand or the sea.

My feelings sad,
And my conscience mad,
I go to bed and rest my head.

I wake up myself,
It is hard to find,
Myself as I cannot see myself,
I looked at the sun too long,

I am now registered blind.

Parental Advisory

Explicit Content.
€#¢∞§¶•ᵃᵒᵃ•¶§∞#¢∞§¶•ᵃᵒ—ᵃ¶§∞#¢∞§¶•ᵃᵒ—≠—
ᵒᵃ•¶§∞¢#¢∞§¶•ᵃᵒ—ᵒᵃ•¶§∞¢#¢∞§¶•ᵃᵒ—≠—
ᵒᵃ•¶§∞¢#¢∞§¶^¨†ƒᵃ~≤ᵒπø¨√∫´©´~¬…øᵃ•¶´∂~∞¢
#´Δ°øᵃ´ƒ¶©§∞®¢√∫~¬πᵃ•¶§∞¢´´Δ°¬πᵃ•´©∞¢®ƒ~
©´Δ´§¬¨øππᵒᵃ∞¢¢´´Δ°≤µ~ƒ∂´¶"≠—
ᵒ¨ᵃ•¶§~†≤®∞¨´#¢•ᵃ¨ᵒ∫~"…¬°~√¨®¥°…¬ƒ∂ç√∫~¬øᵃ
¨¶†§®´∑ †≈ç¥√~π≤µ~¨®´®¬¨^æ…æ456572124
æ°…´ƒ∂ßœ´Δ°§••#¢∞§

Personal Hygiene

The notice above the urinal said:
'Now wash your hands.'
But as there was no one else around,
To set a good example to,
I didn't bother.

The Reflection Pool

I see my reflection,
Upon the reflection pool,
It amazes me so I look,
Some more and see no whirlpool,

The reflection is still,
So crystal clear,
Reflected light without a spill,
I can see a reflection as smooth as a sphere.

How now forehead?
This pool reminds me of you,
As the moon sleeps, I go to bed,
Humanity rests and the owl view.

The sun shineth upon thy head,
The light is bright; it blindeth men.
Light is upon the room, is this our doom?
The light builds up and men leave the room.

THE INTERPRETATION
COLLECTION

Tables

Tables are fascinating,
And if you shift the s to the start,
JESUS!
There he was born.

Meaning

What is the meaning,
Of the meaning of mean?
What hath the meanings
Of mean beholdeth?
Is it the mean of four, five and six?
Or did I mean to do that?
All I know is that this means that,
Mean is a mean meaning for a word.

Save the Trees

ok.

Layered Dream

I was born in a house,
Is a song by Johaan Strauss,
Said the man to the dog,
In a book,
In a film,
In my dream that happened last night,
Said my friend who was born in a house,
Is a song by Johaan Strauss,
In a dream I had.

A Sad Story

A sad story,
Not in this book.

Parrot

There was once a parrot,
There was once a parrot,
Oh, clearly there still is.

Question

How could you?
Where do you draw the line?

Here:

____

Punchline

Things build up,
Things go fine,
They are all building towards,
The main punchline.
Some poems here,
Don't have it;
Be careful with your hopes.

THE MUNDANE DAILY
EXPERIENCE COLLECTION

Calm Under Pressure

I wake up in the morning,
And I feel fresher,
As yesterday I went,
To calm under pressure.

Records

I set a world record,
And the record was,
Eating the most biscuits on a runway in
Denmark from 4am to 4:15am while hanging
upside down.

I also set another one,
I greeted the greatest number of people on the
London Underground on a Sunday morning
when I wasn't in London (I was on the phone to
them).

And I threw the most darts in one minute while
sitting without a belt on in a helicopter.

I am a record player and I've set the world
record for the most amount of world records
while a parrot approaches me.

World records,
World records,
World records.

Autocorrect

Doy yoy knoy hoy loyng it toyk moy toy wroyte this quoyschun in loweecase withoyte it auitocorrecying?

Whu oj whu arf thrse wlrds nod aitocortecting?

Maybe my phone is stuck on a Northern Irish keyboard.

Going to Subway

What bread do you want?
Now, half a foot or a foot?
'Heartfelt Corn Roll' is a good choice,
Or our new 'Seeded Sociality'?
Cheese and toasted?
Okay sure, Spicy cheese,
Normal cheese, or Bonjour Cheese?
Bonjour cheese is like normal cheese but it's
Frenchly served on a slightly different bread
Type -
'Baguette Monsieur' -
Salad?
We have no sweetcorn.
Sauce?
Spicy sauce?
Sorry, it' an extra charge to put that sauce with
'Baguette Monsieur'
The drink is about 15p,
Cookies?

The Making of IKEA

So chaps,
Let's first make our shop more like a;
Labyrinth.
All our products come with booklets -
You're doomed without one,
And probably with one too.
Let's put the Café at the end,
And call all our products;
'Djörk'

Stationery

I see a man,
And he gives me a fan,
But it does not please me.

I see a piece of paper and it was stationary.
It pleased me.

Stationary stationery pleases me.

Four Types

There are Four Types of people in this world.
Those who pronounce it
'En-ve-lope'
And those who say 'On-Vuh-Lope'
And the weird man in the corner who says
"invillip,"
And the French people who think they are the
same.

Feel the Fear and Do it
Anyway

Embrace the fear,
Have confidence.
Believe in yourself,
Then run away.

THE FOOD COLLECTION

The Shop

Once upon a day,
Located in May,
I went to a shop,
To buy a lollipo-
"YOU OKAY?"
I also bought a bottle,
It was a bott-
"POUND PLEASE THANKS BYE"

Wibble

I sometimes sit, and wonder where I
would dibble,
If jelly, such a thing, had less of a
wibble.
I would browse it for sure,
I would eat it much more,
Without a wibble, it deserves a nibble.

The Toughest Question

Hello,
It is good to see you again:

You've overcome the biggest
dilemmas,
You've battled the toughest
enemies,
You've trialled the trials,
Battled the battles,
Fought the fights,
And Englished the Chilean.
You've come such a long way.
So,
Would you like a nibble?

Munch

I just ate something,
It made a crunch,
I guess that qualifies my action as a munch.
I ate another thing,
It didn't make a crunch,
I guess that means
I chewed it.

THE BRUMMIE COLLECTION

(please forgive me if you find this collection
weird.

Kind regards,

Steve.)

Steve's Jobb

Steve had a jobb,
He worked for an apple,
Maple Syrup,
On an apple,
Pick a beer up.

S Word

Don't say this word,
It's very rude,
You might even get,
Told off by some dude,
The word is slemanchè.
Worry not,
Say Steve you can,
Pick up a slemanching beer.

Steveashstios

Posh Greek Steve,
Has this name,
If say something different,
You'll just be playing silly games.
Steveashstios eats Greek Yoghurt,
Low Fat, Greek, Yoghurt,
Steveashstios,
Have yourself a feta,
Pick up a Greek Style Beer.

Stoive

Brum brum in me car,
Stoive is listening to Andrew Marr,
Bostin,
We're not in Boston,
Stoive had a beer.

Steve

What a heave,
Mr Steve,
This is the greatest,
From our latest,
Steve, heave Steve heave.
Drain the keg,
Drink the beer.

Steve Weave

Steve is a spider.
So he deployed his glider,
To pick a beer, any beer.

Steve had a Beard

Then he shaved.
And picked up a beer.

BEER

Pickup one Pickup one Pickup one Pickup one
Pickup one Pickup one Pickup one Pickup one
Pickup one Pickup one Pickup one Pickup one
Pickup one Pickup one Pickup one Pickup one
Pickup one Pickup one Pickup one Pickup one
Pickup one Pickup one Pickup one Pickup one
Pickup one Pickup one Pickup one Pickup one
Pickup one Pickup one Pickup one Pickup one

Pickup one  Pickup one
Pickup one Pickup one
Pickup one Pickup one
Pickup one Pickup one
Pickup one Pickup one
Pickup one Pickup one
Pickup one Pickup one
Pickup one Pickup one
Pickup one Pickup one

Pickup one Pickup one Pickup one Pickup one
Pickup one Pickup one Pickup one Pickup one
Pickup one Pickup one Pickup one Pickup one
Pickup one Pickup one Pickup one Pickup one
Pickup one Pickup one Pickup one Pickup one
Pickup one Pickup one Pickup one Pickup one
Pickup one Pickup one Pickup one Pickup one
Pickup one Pickup one Pickup one Pickup one
Pickup one Pickup one Pickup one Pickup one
Pickup one Pickup one Pick oh, Pick one up.

THE GRAND COLLECTION

Going Dutch

I heard on a medical programme on Radio 4,
Of a disturbing syndrome thaat afflicts some
stroke sufferers,
That on recovery they find themselves talking
with a foreign accent,
This hasn't happened to me – at least not when
I taalk,
But when I type, some of the words look
decijedly Dutch.
'Doouble Dutch, more lijke,'
My son qujipped.
But I dijdn't think ijt funny.
I waas worrijed;
In fact, I had just decijec to go and see the
doctor.
But my son said to check first with PC World.

Beijing Butterfly

In Dave's word processor manual it warned:
**Never touch the magnetic surface of the
disk!**
Underneath was a diagram of a man's hand,
touching it.
But a big cross was superimposed
To show that he shouldn't.

Dave developed a sneaking regard
For the reckless man
Whose hand it was.

One day when his wife was out
And he had nothing left to process,
Dave impulsively brushed his finger
Across the magnetic surface of the disk.
Nothing happened.
He applied more pressure - nothing.
A dud, probably.
He went through all his disks
First touching then pressing then rubbing.
Again nothing.

But the next morning there was a transport
strike,
Which paralysed the whole of France.

Irresponsibility

Colin had had too much to drink
So decided to go home on the bus.
He sat down near the front.
But the driver beckoned
And silently pointed
To a machine.
Colin sluggishly caught on
And tried to insert a fiver.
The driver shook his head.
Colin hesitated, then put in a pound.
The driver tapped his fingers impatiently
Then pointed to a sign:
Night Service £1.50.
Colin put in another pound,
And waited for his ticket to emerge.
But nothing happened.
The driver looked heavenwards,
As if seeking help;
Then pointed to another machine,
From which a ticket was sticking out.
Colin pulled but it tore in half.
Then he waited for his change,
But the driver waved him away
And said to the next passenger,
'See that?
Absolutely Incapable!
He's on no fit state to be on a bus;
Should have stuck to his car.'

There is a poem here,
But it is in white font.

Fireworks For Cats

In the cat section of Pet World,
They have everything imaginable for cats.
For example, there are eight types of cat flap;
Some manual, others magnetic or electronic -
Two with remote controls.
I chose an electronic one with a remote control,
In burnt spice to match the back door.

Waiting with this,
And other cat purchases at the
Check-out,
I suddenly exclaimed,
'Gosh, look, *they're* new;
What will they think of next?
They've got special fireworks for cats over
there!'
Half the queue eagerly rushed off
Leaving me feeling rather foolish
As I'd only said it as a joke.

Tipp-Tack

When Blu-Tack and Tipp-Ex came out
I used to get them mixed up.
All my visual aids fell off the classroom wall,
And the Headmaster returned my reports
With a terse note complaining they were lumpy.

Trouble with Mice

'We are relocating,' said the notice in the
stationer's window.
The new store was entirely different
And was called 'Stationery City,'
With piped rock music playing;
And new staff
Who kept saying, 'No problem.'
The manager said, 'What do you think?'
'Mmm, okay, but isn't the music rather…?'
'No problem. You don't notice it after a bit.
Have you seen our promotional offer?'

It was by the entrance,
'It's a correction mouse,' said the girl,
'If you buy one you get
The highlighter mouse for half price.'
'Why mice?' I asked.
'It's just a rational ergonomic design solution
really
That turned out looking like a mouse.
But they're quite cute and funky, don't you
think?
And if you buy now,
You get a mouse pad free.'

Later in the pub,
I couldn't work out the connection
Between the mouse pad
And the correction and highlighter mice.
Then I trailed the highlighter across the pad,

Then corrected it.

A lad with a Budweiser was watching.
I asked him:
'No mate; your pad's for your mouse.'
'Which one?'
'Not *those*: your PC mouse, yeah?'
'Oh right, cheers.'
'No problem.'

Döppelganger

In town today five people
Asked for my autograph
Thinking I was Freddie Mercury.
It's always happening.

My friends are skeptical.
'But you are totally unlike him
In every way possible!'

'Quite!'
That's exactly what *they* say!
More or less.
They say, "Gosh, you look totally different
From when you're on the telly:
Must be down to special lighting
Camera angles
And make-up."

Replacement Cat Flap

I needed a new cat flap
As the electronic one from Pet World
Had got permanently stuck in the
'No entry from outside' mode,
And the cat had broken the remote control.
I went to the local pet shop this time.
They only had the one type:
Manually controlled and in dull grey.
'It will tone in nice with any decor,' said the
man.
I pretended to agree.
Anyway, it would make a change,
From burnt spice.

Inside the package
Were the installation instructions.
But first it said:

Our compliments on your discernment and
taste in purchasing this quality product from
Petsmate™

For the rest of the day my mum kept asking,
'Why have you got that silly smug smile on your
face?'

Early Days

'What do you do?' asked the man at the party.

'I am a poet,' I replied.

'And what sort of things do you write about?'

'Oh; towers, toes, makeshift housing, shoes,
pyjamas,
And zebras.'

'Real thought-provoking stuff, then?'

'Ha, well…
No, but I thought that I ought to start simply
Then gradually work my way up to, er, that sort
of thing,'

'You haven't been a poet long, then?'

'Three weeks this coming Saturday.'

'Can you really call yourself a poet
After only three weeks, then?'

'Well, I think it's best to establish
That you are one from the outset, really.'

'Mmm.'

'Well. it might cause less confusion later.'

'Oh?'

'I mean, say my collected works
Came out in ten years' time
And I wrote in the introduction:
"I have been a poet for ten years
Except for the first three weeks, that is,"
Wouldn't it sound a bit well…
D'you know what I mean?'

THE PROBLEMS COLLECTION

Sorry

“I kicked the ball in your face,
 Sorry,”
“Stop saying sorry!”
“Sorry.”

Open The Front Door

I've been waiting out here hours!
C'mon!
Open it,
I know you're in the shower but like,
Put a towel on,
I need to enter.

Take Ur Shooze Off

Don't worry about it,
No, no, don't worry I'll take them off,
Honestly, don't make a fit,
Really, I want to take them off,
It's cold in the house though,
But I might get your carpet dirty,
Ok, go
Ahead, ya piece of shoff.

Missing the Train

Oh no! Oh my gosh!
I missed the train!
No! *puff*
I'll just have to wait for the next one,
Argh,
There's loads of people on the next one!
TEN WHOLE MINUTES, I'm not standing for
this,
I'm going to email the manager,
And tell them the train came 20 seconds too
early.

No More Milk

I want to indulge in some cereal,
But I can't;
'Make sure there's enough left for my cup of
tea!'
Why, Oh, Why?
What pleasure can your caffeine bring,
Which the cereal cannot surpass?

Batteries

'I need some batteries from the cupboard.'
'What type?
AA - easy, got loads.
AAA - Probably.
The Square Ones - Seasonal Stock.
Round Ones - Not. A. *CHANCE!*'

Weekday Wake Up

It's the weekend!
I can lie in, I can relax,
I can have a big breakfast.
I will now check my phone.
A text.
WHY ARE YOU NOT HERE YET, IT'S 2PM.
IT'S MONDAY.

Purpose Built Factory

"Why does he spend so much time in there?"

"Well,
Donkeys will always kick,
And chickens will always cluck."

"I hereby accept the issue."

THE ILLUSTRATED COLLECTION

Moo The Kangaroo

The Bingo Dingo

Perry the Punk

Absolute,
Rebel.

Shopping Dilemma

Bob from Windows XP

Peter The Potato

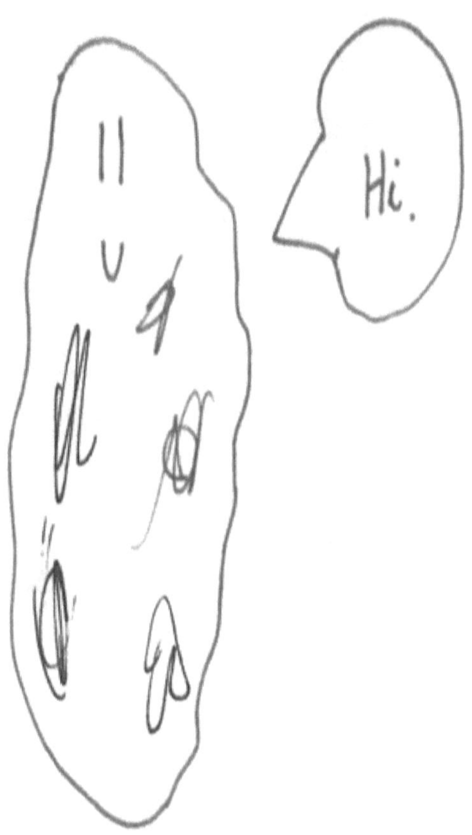

Save The Trees 2

Behold,

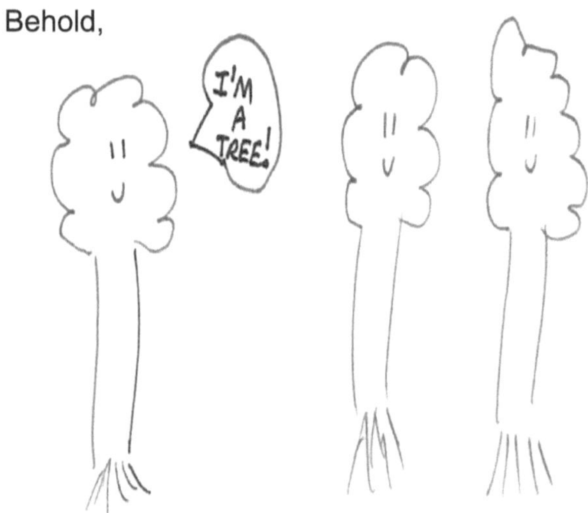

Adhere to thy sacred trees,
For every book produced,
Three trees,
Planted right here.

OOGA DOOGA

THE ANIMAL COLLECTION

Embarrassed Son

Cat sat on mat,
Matt sat on cat,
Cat splat on Mat,
Matt's not my dad.

Parrot *Parrot*

There was once a parrot.
There was once a parrot.
Still he liv'th.

Chihuahua

I was born next to a zoo,
And since the nurse was a kangaroo,
I wonder to this day,
Which cage I shall be one day be placed,
But alas!
I once spoke to a lion,
And it said to me,
"Roaarr".

Dragons' Pen

Don't let the dragons out their pen,
Even if they make you an offer,
Deborzebra peadon someone,
Toucan Suliman,
Was a very silliman,
Jennyfish Campbell,
Was a very camp bell.
Penguin Jones,
Ran from the rolling boulder.
Dingo Bannatyne,
Wanted to advertise,
'It's banner time!'
He said.

So,
Um…
Yeah.

THE SIT YOURSELF BACK AND RELAX BECAUSE THERE IS A LOT TO READ COLLECTION

Australian

Guddoy, moyte.

Borus

Johstoñ.

Picnic

Did you bring the cheese?

Say that again?

Don't mumble this time please.

Something Scary

Something scarier.

Thump In The Dump

There goes my old sofa.

Bubbles

Pop. Pop, pop;
Pop.

Small Car Bob

I tried to get in a car but,
I didn't fit;
For it was made of leg..oh

A Good Song Comes On In The Car

Crank it up Dave.

Sequel

This is the sequel,
Chiasmus be the prequel,
Next year you might get the treacle.

New Song

I just listened to a new song.
It's a classic.

Cheese on Beans or Beans on Cheese

It's Beans on Cheese,
You ¡€#¢∞§¶•ªº∂!

Rallentando

Slowwwwwwwwwwwwwwwww
DOWWWNNNNNNNN

O
K
A
Y

T
H
E
N

French Fri

I am currently travelling to a shop,
 Looking for its sign with my eye
  So I can buy a French
Fri.

Short Poem

This is a short poem.
I can guarantee you that,
You might see Richard the third,
Wearing a top hat,

This is the second paragraph,
Not as short as you thought,
Wondering how long,
Left until the end is brought,

You saw this title,
And wanted a short poem,
You are questioning the length,
But it's more like a hymn,

I will let you go now,
This poem is not bad,
It wasn't very short,
But by reading, you are glad!

Microphone

Testing,
Testing,
123.

Fairground Ride

Sorry mate,
It's broken down.

Gastronomy

Wait isn't that about space or sump'n.

Quad Colon

I came; I saw; I conquered;
I apologised.

Nationalisation

Would you like a cup of tea?

THE COLLECTION OF SOME IMPORTANCE

Love My Lithp

Thith Poem ith good,
And now i have a quethton,
Do I have a lithp,
Or do i thpeak like thith,
Itth you, the audienth who getth to dethide,
Tho go fors,
And tell me thath you think what you think of my
lithp.

Question

Which copy of Chiasmus do you own?
The one with the red underline?
A signed copy?
Alternate cover version?
A not-for-resale version?
Doesn't matter,
For it might one day be worth a fortune.

Yoga

I wake up in the morning,
And do some yoga,
And then see my Latin teacher,
Wearing a toga.

I get home in the evening,
And turn into a cook,
Then I see the teacher,
Reading a Latin book.

Dative case, is on the casus,
In briefca(s)e do up your laci,
Although you don't havebam any,
You are Wareing a toga.

Complexities and consequences of daily subconscious action

Think think think,
Don't you shrink,
But consequently,
But super relentlessly,
Bears. Cares,
Shares in companies.

Modern life,
Tife and strife,

I play my piano,
All day long,
But it doesn't make a sound.

Oh dear.

Your Poem

Once upon a time,
There was a __________, quite sublime,
Who wanted to go to _________,
His _______ didn't agree,
Got _______ by a bee,
And found a big ____ to climb.

______ fell out the _____
Oh dearie me!
How could you even grasp it?
So he saw his _______ twice,
Got ________ by some mice,
And went off happily.

Gluestick

There's nothing more satisfying,
Than a new glue stick,
And nothing more scary,
Than that guy John Wick,

I sit in geography,
Pondering life,
And think how might use this gluestick,
Full of energy and strife,

Then suddenly the sheet comes round,
And someone takes my gluestick,
They squish it hard into the paper,
And it makes the paper soggy,
My life has been ruined.

My hand falls off,
The world ends,
I can no longer stick my sheet in,
Cause my hand is no longer bonger.

Joke

Knock Knock,
Who's there?
Bald man,
Bald man who?
Bald man don't know.

Fourty

I turned fourty,
But everyone laughed, when I texted them that,
I guess they're just jealous,
That I am Fourty,
Or maybe it's frustration,
That I'm allways corecting there speeling.

Song

ououOuOuOUOU
La La La
HAHAHA
LaLaLa
HAHAHA
YAWOWOWOW
HAHAHA
HAHAHA

Canadian Horse

A normal horse,
But from Canada,
Meaning it might be a little larger.
And it won't have seen London.

Wishing

When you wish upon a star,
You'll probably burn because they're super-hot;
So I think I'd rather not.

Maybe wish upon the moon,
For your dream might come true.
Especially if your dream was to visit the moon.

Theory

The Earth is flat.
Australia doesn't exist.
The Queen is a multiple of four.
Steven Spielberg is actually Ed Sheeran.
France is Spanish.
Santander bank was founded in a toilet.
Theory of knowledge,
How do you know the K is silent?
Chiasmus is a good book.

THE EPIC POEM SAGA

Larkin Edmond Jones I: Oh Tidings Of Bleak

Edmond,
Thy Larkin of Jones,
Land from the sky unto cæmon,
Into thus moans,

On our Mundane,
And Welsh,
England he hath be on Monday,
Forth where it shall be time for the great mesh,
Of forces a war,
A war,
A *war*–
Masses, destruction it is to be,
It will be tore,
Into the heart of the land of he.

Larkin Edmond Jones II: Freeze and Thaw

The journey,
Nigh; what a rock,
Only,
The ever-relentless power of nature,
Into the crack with expansion,
Breaking apart the tribe,

Weather,
Nature,
Life,
God,

Oh, have mercy on the legion,
Free us,
Free them,
Free yourself.

Larkin Edmond Jones III: The Great Batheticist

Bathetic,
Such a feat
Of great slick,

The unintentional,
The sadness,
The prevailing gloominess of the past,

Oh,
How bleak, unsurprising of cheat,
Oh,
How Larkin last,
Not like math but
Alas!
I never was prepared through my cheated life:
I hath noth hath thath wrath.

Thighan Howercawldson I: A Man of Honour

His sword was of power,
His statue a tower,
Of the brushed-up wind of the land.
But his mind was unclear,
He couldn't pick up more than a beer,
And stuck his potential within the sand.

A man of honour he was,
He knew the Lethoskopical Toz,
The highly-held king of the shores,
He had won many a battle,
Been awarded many a cattle,
And was too humble to receive applause.

He was went away,
At a time located in May,
To win a war for his soil,
He prepared for this feat,
He knew not to cheat,
For it would be a lot of long toil.

Thighan Howercawldson II: Preparation

An unsheathing of glisten,
Would make the enemy listen,
To any word he may have to say,
The silver, strong sword,
Had come out of its hoard,
And Thighan was ready to play.

He placed on his shoes,
Shook off all the booze,
And took a moment to pray.
Then he turned to his friend,
Said: 'This will be the end
Of the enemy and their king, today'.

The time is 9:02,
You have one hour.
Off you go, Thighan,
And good luck on your battle.
May you win.

Thighan Howercawldson III: Wind O' The West

His prophecies are unforetold,
The tale of old,
It withstand'th the enemy anwealda,
Acwellan happen today, oh Huthman.
He speak'th baldlice,
Ye onfon,
Ye onfon of s'pport.
The wielding undertaken health,
'To the Sky!'
They cry.
WEST is the way forward,
For EAST, SOUTH, AND NORTH,
May tha'y thus not r'main.
For SOUTH is of ev'l,
NORTH the strongholds of the anwealda.
WEST is the way,

Thighan,
With an unsheathing,
Regains the soil by blood,
And cold mercy.

Finale

Thighan you are – you are Larkin,
Hello, my friend.
Welcome to my castle.
We have won.
It is good to see you again:

You've overcome the biggest dilemmas,
You've battled the toughest enemies,
You've trialled the trials,
And battled the battles,
Fought the fights,
And Larkin'd the Edmonds.
You've come such a long way.
So,
Would you like sugar in ya cup o' tea?

THE THROWAWAY COLLECTION

(Stuff that didn't make the main book, but I guess it did)

Lace In Ya Face

Walking home,
Walking to school,
Running a lap,
Round the
swimming pool.

Lace comes
undone,
Fall over John,
They're dirty now,
I can't be bothered to do them back up.

But there is a solution,
Let's take off the shoe,
So both my feet are unsheathed,
And fall in the pool.

Under the Pillow

I hide my strawberries,
Under the pillow,
Just in case.

Fortnite

I played a game one day,
That day isn't today,
I wanted to play that game,
The game was Mario,
I played it a fortnight ago.

Lorsque Porque

I have strings,
You can play me,
My style can change,
And many of you have a specific taste.
I'm popular round the world,
Because the thought of me sounds sweet.
Music to your ears, but,
What am I?

Not a guitar,
I am a game that you can play with stringy
cheese.

Pigeon

One day I sent a pigeon,
To go on a mission,
It underwent fission,
And brought back a lemon,
Thanks.
I sent another pigeon,
With another mission,
And it successfully competethed.

However,
I amn't happy with pigeon.
For it left a mark on my windscreen,
Thanks.

Reverse Meanings

I have un tableau de chocolat.
Chocolate bar, or six-pack?
They are quite the opposite,
But have the same name.
Reminds me of something else:
Coronation Street.

Stephen Mulhern

Some things boil,
And some things turn,
But there is only one,
Stephen Mulhern.

Core-Bin

You might choose to vote for the core-bin,
Not the silly bin,
The month is May,
You may vote for that,
Maybe for the 'surgeon,
Or the 'Farrage.'

They do it different in Solihull

I was at a vending machine
But it didn't vend,
Instead, it punched me,
I was at a sink
But it extracted the water from my hand
I bought a drink
But it made me dehydrated.
I went to a football match,
But it took place in a ring and they wore gloves.
I got given a book
But I couldn't read it.
They do it different in Solihull.

Campfire

I have always wondered,
And pondered,
Why my campfire,
I always so cheerful,
It's cause it's a *camp*fire.

Animal Atrocity

The cow said meow,
Got famous,
Cow said ow,
No longer famous.

Oh no I spilt a glass

Of water.
I'll clean it up,
I will,
Not today,
Oh wait, it evaporates,
I'll do it now.

Freddie Jupiter

Is this the real life,
Is this just fantasy,
Born in a planet,
With no escape from gravity.

Brian July comes along,
With his guitar solo,
But he gets crushed by the gravity.

Buying a new table

What colour do you want?
I'd recommend 'Posh Burgundy',
It's actually the only one we haven't sold out of,
It's nice,
It even comes with the optional removable bit in
the middle,
Innovative.
How much?
599, reduced to 499.
It'll make you knock - -
On wood.

Croque-Monsieur

I went to a cafè,
And guess what I saw?
It was a beautiful,
'Croque-Monsieur'
It was behind the counter,
I ordered a copy,
I like to eat photos.

Photos are delish,
I take the photo,
And it makes a click,
The flash of the light,
Purely asserts what it is,

There is one small problem,
There are so many of them,
There is no time,
So put on some lemon and lime,
And eat 'em.

Joke 2

This book.
As in, it contains jokes;
Do you get me?
You might be confused,
I could be asking if you understand,
Or, if you get me and that I'm a joke.
Confusion.
Your choice.

END OF POEMS

TOTAL PAGES FOR THE POEMS: 127

CHECK THAT YOU HAVE READ EACH POEM THOROUGHLY AND CHECKED THROUGH THEM CAREFULLY.

Time for some celebration.

Here are some bits and bobs.

ACKNOWLEDGEMENTS

Poems from 'The Grand Collection' written by Michael Richardson, as well as 'Personal Hygiene.'

Many thanks to Luke Sterry, who contributed 'Short Poem' and 'The Sun' to the book.

Gratefulness towards Kiran Sodha, Who helped with the cover and the tweaking of many poems within.

Thank you to everybody who picked up a copy of *Chiasmus;* you probably regret it.

To the people of King Edwards School - Birmingham, for inspiring many of the things within these pages.

To the inventor of paper, as this book would not be possible without its presence.

To Amazon, for accepting our book, And the rainforest for providing the trees.

To everyone who read this book, especially those who did so word-for-word.

To ourselves, for creating such a
masterpiece.

So, that's the acknowledging done.
This book took a while to make,
So, please don't try this at home.

See you with what's next….

MATERIALISM

Our Books Are on Amazon
Including the first book, Chiasmus;
On every countrys' amazons.

WARNING: IF YOU'RE IN BRAZIL, DON'T GO TO THE RAINFOREST.

For merchandise or book copies (including signed) go to:

OHDEARME.BIGCARTEL.COM
(Subject, but unlikely, to change. Correct as of the release of this book)

STATISTICS

The number of A's in this book: 1863
The number of B's in this book: 485
The number of C's in this book: 777
The number of D's in this book: 869
The number of E's in this book: 2914
The number of F's in this book: 481
The number of G's in this book: 476
The number of H's in this book: 1375
The number of I's in this book: 1722
The number of J's in this book: 58
The number of K's in this book: 445
The number of L's in this book: 922
The number of M's in this book: 627
The number of N's in this book: 1735
The number of O's in this book: 2220
The number of P's in this book: 701
The number of Q's in this book: 36
The number of R's in this book: 1284
The number of S's in this book: 1441
The number of T's in this book: 2220
The number of U's in this book: 883
The number of V's in this book: 182
The number of W's in this book: 503
The number of X's in this book: 38
The number of Y's in this book: 591
The number of Z's in this book: 15

The number of words in this book: 6173

The number of pages in this book: 150

The number of letters in the alphabet: 26

The number of people who composed the book: 2

The number of trees wasted for the book:
None, since loads were planted in the
illustrated collection.

The number of words in the statistics section: 289

The number of Steve's in this book: 24

The number of characters in this book in tally
form excluding this tally (34543):

NOTES:

NOTES:

NOTES:

NOTES:

Theory 2

I have a theory,
You may have the the query,
'What is this theory?'
You see,
Every time you finish a book,
You should take a look,
At this theory.
At the end of a book,
Just before you've quitted,
Make sure you've omitted,
An E.
But don't worry,
You didn't notice the extra 'the,'
Thend.